How to Get an Audible Version

of Your Book
2nd Edition

Updated Version

How to For You Series #22

Dorothy May Mercer

ISBN 13: 978-1-62329-093-1
ISBN 10: 1-62329-093-7

© Copyright 2016, 2021
Updated 2021
Mercer Publications & Ministries, Inc.
Stanwood, Michigan U.S.A.

Table of Contents

Introduction *1*

The Audible Web Site *2*

Be Your Own Producer? *4*

Investments vs. Profits? *5*

Royalties *6*

Audible Customer Reviews *9*

    A Few Drawbacks **9**

CD—Compact Disk or DVD? *11*

Split Royalty *13*

    The Try-Out Sample **13**

Auditions & Messages *15*

    Messages **15**

    Auditions **16**

Choosing a Producer *19*

Make an Offer *21*

    Price Per Finished Hour **21**

    Due Date for the First Fifteen Minutes **22**

Locked/Unlocked *23*

    Final Due Date **24**

Creating a Cover *25*

    Uploading Your Cover 27

Corrections and Changes..*28*

Downloading a Sample *29*
    External Storage..29
    Horror Stories 29

   How to Download...**30**
    How to Move 31
    Creating a New Folder 33
    How to Drag and Drop 33

Relaxing the Rules, in Practice.....................................*34*

Some Are Perfectionists *35*

The Retail Sample *36*

Final Approval & Payment *38*

Joilè!...*39*

Marketing...*40*

Introduction

This booklet will explain how to have your book recorded on Audible.com, which is a subsidiary of Amazon.com. It will tell you a little bit about my experience with Audible, as well.

Navigating the ACX.com web site, like any new thing, is a learning experience. At first, I said some naughty words under my breath, but now it is easy. This booklet will help you with that as well as give you some valuable tips. Be aware that I use a desktop computer with a Windows operating system. If your system is different you may be able to adapt any detailed directions as needed.

The Audible Web Site

The Audible web site (ACX.com) is designed with two major pathways:
1.) Producers (Narrators)
2.) Authors as Rights Owners.

Assuming you are in category two, the author and rights owner, first you go to ACX.com and set up an author's account, the same as any other site. You will be invited to enter your personal information, address, email address, tax information, bank information and password. You may use your Amazon ID and password, if you want. Forever after, you will find the "Log In" words somewhere in upper level of your Audible Home screen. They may even call you by your author name, as in "Welcome Dorothy May Mercer," but you still have to log in to do anything important. At some point, you may allow them to recognize your computer, in which case you can bypass the log-in step. Nevertheless, it is a good idea to remember your ID and password.

The home page of the web site is made up of interesting information about the company and how it works, with links to many helpful articles.

However the important portals for you, as the author, will be across the top. After the welcome words you will find *Projects, Auditions, New Messages, Account Settings* and *Add Your Title*. Click on any of these and you will be asked to enter your ID and password. Click Submit and you will be taken to the right department. (Note: After the site starts to recognize you, and you have an Audible recording for sale, these heading may be arranged a bit differently. For example, under your name will be a pulldown menu with: *Add Your Title, View Sales Dashboard, Account Settings, and Logout.*

Assuming you want to get started right away, you click on "Add Your Title". You will be invited to fill in the blanks, with the usual title, links, author, and description. Alternatively, your can enter your book or your author name in a Search area and ACX will bring up a list of items in the Amazon catalog. This description can be copied directly from your Amazon sales page. However, bear in mind you are trying to sell potential narrators, known as "producers," on the merits of your book. And so, you will include the basics as to genre and type of book and then refine that description to include any salient selling points that you have, such as the hundreds or thousands of followers you have on Twitter and Facebook, your best seller rank, the book's high sales rank, and a few quotes from your five star reviews. Try to think of the type of producer you wish to attract and make your best pitch to that producer.

You must mark your choice of man, woman or both, and chose from a list of vocal types. Check off a range that you are willing to pay a producer, per finished hour, in US dollars. The choices are $0 to $50, $50 to $100, $100 to $150, etc. Another option is a split royalty. More on that later.

Be Your Own Producer?

But, wait a minute. Suppose you decide to be your own narrator, that is to narrate your book, yourself. ACX has thought of that, too. They have articles and helps for the self-producer.

I actually briefly thought of doing just that. After all, my voice isn't half bad, I thought, and I had a role in my high-school play. This could be fun. Well, if you have delusions of grandeur, such as I, before you jump off the deep end, do as I did. Consider the idea of a proper recording studio, along with the expensive equipment, and the editing skills required, not to mention the time involved. Spend a little time listening to samples from a few of the top producers. If you still want to do-it-yourself, good luck with that. You are on your own. Check out some of the articles and helps for the self-producer on Audible. The balance of this booklet is concerned with working with a contracted producer.

Investments vs. Profits?

First things first— can I make any money off of it, you ask.

Well, let me ask you this: are you making money off your published books? Audible books are more costly, I think, and require almost as much time. Unless you are J.K. Rowling, or Bill O'Reilly, do it for the glory. You will have to work hard at marketing and promoting and may never get your investment back.

True, there is a different audience for audio books, but those folks are just as savvy and ~~penny-pinching~~ ... er ... wise shoppers as any other. You must break into the market, find a niche, develop a following, and then hope.

We know that "talking books" have been around for a long time, read by volunteers and stuck on library shelves. But it is only in the last five to ten years that Audible.com has made it a big business.

Amazon purchased the company in 2008. In May 2011, when Audible launched Audiobook Creation Exchange (ACX), the company took off.

You may wonder how many Audible books there are. I hesitate to give you numbers as the estimates vary widely. However, today the Audible official site claims to have over 500,000 titles, compared to over thirty million (and growing) total books (of all kinds) on Amazon.

And so, audiobook competition may be less. But, there are fewer prospective audiobook buyers, as well. And so, you make your choice. Is the glory worth the time away from writing, or not?

Royalties

Royalties depend on a couple of factors. The price range of audiobooks can vary greatly, from $12.00 to $35.00, according to the length and popularity.

If you give Audible an exclusive, one-year, sales contract, they will place your book on three outlets (Amazon, iTunes and Audible) and pay you 40% of sales. Unlike Kindle Direct Publishing (KDP.Amazon.com), you do not set the retail price for your book. Audible does. For instance, my novel, *Cynthia and Dan, Cyber War*, was seven hours and fifteen minutes long. I gave Audible an exclusive contract at 40% of sales. Forty percent of Audible's retail price of $17.95 sounds good, doesn't it? At that rate, I thought it shouldn't take long to recover my expenses. As a relatively new Audible author, I searched their web site, in vain, for more details on how the pricing actually worked. I wondered: What exactly is the definition of sales—gross, net, or something else?

It was necessary to wait for my first month's royalty report to learn the unpalatable truth. There were no sales at the retail price. Instead I learned that there are several ways of determining the price, none of which charge the full retail value. There is a plethora of options available. One such program is the Amazon Audible Listener program. For $14.65 a month the customer is allowed one free credit per month which can be used for any item in the Audible catalog. This type of sale garnered a price of $10.37 for which I received $4.15 in royalty. Not too bad.

After a customer has used his one monthly credit, he/she may buy any Audible catalog item for 30% off.

After ninety days he/she has the option to buy bulk credit at another reduced price. This accounts for the great difference in the retail sales prices for which you, as the author, receive a royalty. Another one of my Audible books, *The Fairfax Fix*, retail price $17.53, sold three books under that feature, the first month, grossing $8.93 of which I received $3.57 royalty. Apparently there is more than one price, you see.

As of this writing the Amazon customer has two other membership choices at $7.95 or $22.95 per month. In addition, special sales promotions, and outside competition can affect those prices at any time.

The lowest sales price category on my ACX account sales report was in sales made to customers buying the book who were not in the Audible monthly program—in other words, everyone else. These folks paid a mere $1.99 for which I received a measly $.80 royalty.

The report did not designate whether these sales were made on iTunes, Amazon or Audible. However, my best guess is that it might have been a Kindle reader who bought the eBook and the Audible versions together.

As the owner, once I signed the 40% contract with them, I had no control over the price that Audible placed on the recording. At the end of ninety days, I could opt out of the contract, if I so desired. In that case I could sign a 25% contract with them, giving them a non-exclusive contract. This would allow me to sell the recording anywhere, if I chose to do so.

You see, dear reader, there is a lot to learn and much to consider. It behooves you to research all options.

Let me be clear: I am not accusing Audible of cheating or misrepresenting. They are marketing my product and they did, indeed, pay me 40% of their sales, so far as I know.

After ten years experience with Audible, I can report that, on any one specific book, in general, I receive more on an audible sale than I receive for an Amazon ebook or print book sale, or from the Kindle Edition Normalized Pages (KENP) Read. However, on any one book, there are far fewer Audible sales than eBook sales.

Audible Customer Reviews

In researching for this book, I thought it prudent to read a few reviews, from the customer's point of view.

There are those folks who simply love Audible books. This could be someone who drives a truck or delivery van or has a long commute to work. These folks have discovered that listening to books relieves the boredom and gives them something to look forward to each day.

It could be the houseworker who listens while folding clothes and loading the dishwasher. It could be the patient in a hospital or retirement home. Or just anyone who is tired of TV and computer games, or has tired eyes.

The avid fan has his or her favorite readers, just as you have your favorite authors. Once discovered this fan will devour everything by that reader.

Reviewers agreed that Audible is the gold standard for quality of production. But, some commented that the pricing and distribution system is antiquated. Most of the complaints fell into those two categories.

A Few Drawbacks

On the negative side were those disgruntled customers who had a bad experience and swore off Audible for good. A couple of folks had started with the free thirty day offer, and tried to cancel, only to be billed for the second month's service. The complaints were resolved to their satisfaction. However, this illustrates the type of accounting errors one might encounter with any new and growing company. The recommendation is, if you, as a customer, decide to cancel, allow plenty of time for your cancelation to hit their billing department.

From our standpoint, as authors, ten years ago, when I started, the worst news was from those customer/reviewers who praised the generous return policy. I was shocked to learn that the customer thinks he has a full year to listen to the book, decide he doesn't like it and return it for credit. I shuddered to think of receiving unlimited chargebacks anytime up to a year, but in ten years I only had two Audible books returned. Fortunately, Audible has now addressed this problem. The customers' benefits are still generous. But, as of January 1, 2021, Audible is paying me full royalties on any book return made more than seven days after purchase. Also, they pay so much per page read on any book returned in less than seven days.

Moving on, this booklet is about getting an Audible version of your book and not, necessarily, an instruction book on how customers can beat the system.

CD—Compact Disk or DVD?

Audible does not make a CD. They only market the online recordings in MP3 format for computer and Bluetooth players. And so, if you want to manufacture a CD you must give Audible a non-exclusive contract, meaning you can sell your Audible book in other places and manufacture a CD, if you want. Audible will still place your Audible book on the same three aforementioned outlets, but now they will pay you only 25% of sales.

Matter of fact, I tried doing that with one of my novels. After putting it on a non-exclusive contract with Audible, I thought I could manufacture and market my audiobooks myself. It's a long story. Indeed, I learned to make the discs, but totally failed at marketing them. For your edification, entertainment, and amusement, I shall digress for a few paragraphs. Here is the story:

I soon discovered that CDs do not carry enough minutes to hold my novel. The maximum is eighty minutes of sound. My novel was seven and a half hours, or 450 minutes, meaning it would require six CDs to record. If you have ever looked at audio books in a public library you will see what I mean. And so, I investigated using DVDs, instead. One DVD would hold my entire novel. And so, I invested in 100 writable DVD discs, the necessary containers, as well as all the paraphernalia and software required to make the colorful labels and covers.

My anticipation knew no bounds as I waited for all this stuff to be delivered. When it arrived I tore open the packages, happy as a field mouse in a harvest bin.

Soon, I was busy reading instructions and installing software on my computer. The hours and days flew by as I immersed myself in my favorite activity–creating.

As you may have guessed, one thing called for another as expenses mounted. But the happy day came when I completed my first DVD, shrink-wrapped it with a copy of the print book, and took it to my local retail outlet's book sales display.

Not every endeavor is destined for success, as you know. Perhaps I should have considered that not all CD players will also play a DVD. One needs a DVD player, or a combination player. Automobile CD players do not play DVDs.

Months later the book plus DVD was gathering dust, still awaiting its first sale. Surely, I needed a better marketing plan.

There is a company that markets Audible books to libraries. And so, I applied to them. But they needed a list of my catalog of dozens of Audible CDs and DVDs. Clearly, one was not enough. They never responded.

At that time, I had no further marketing plan and so, I moved on.

I hope you enjoyed the story, and so we shall return to the discussion of getting an Audible recording for your book.

Split Royalty

You may choose to offer your book on a split royalty basis. Rather than offering to pay a certain amount per finished hour, you agree to split the royalty with the producer, usually on a 50-50 basis.

Oftentimes, a new author will offer his/her book for a split royalty, thinking to save money. Theoretically, splitting the royalties will work, however do not expect to attract experienced producers. Sometimes producers who are trying to break into the field will start with a split royalty deal, to establish a reputation and gain experience. If your book is a true best-seller, no doubt there will be great producers falling over themselves to record your book. However, the rest of us can expect to prove that old saw, "You get what you pay for."

The Try-Out Sample

Finally, you upload an excerpt from your book for potential producers to read and record as a try-out. The easy way is to copy the first few paragraphs from your book, but there is a better way. It takes a bit of time, but I recommend choosing a variety of passages that will showcase the producer's different voices. At a minimum you want to hear how he/she sounds as narrator, male hero, female heroine and the bad guy. If possible, go a

13

step further and include, for example, an accented voice, a child, and an elderly person. You could include a bit of a fight scene and an intimate scene or a group scene where lots of people are talking. Include as much variety as possible, within the limit of 2000 characters allowed.

A good producer will be able to change his/her voice to reflect the different characters, their emotions, and the particular action involved. There are a few famous authors who have Hollywood celebrities read their books. Others have several people on the recording. But we mortals do not have that kind of money.

There is a separate space provided for your directions. It is helpful to give the potential producers ideas as to how this should be read. For instance, you might point out the type of character this is, such as shrill, relaxed, sexy, young excited, laid back. Or you might describe the scene, such as, "this scene is the climax of the book where the Martians are about to annihilate the whole town, etc." Put yourself in the position of directing the scene.

Once you are satisfied, submit your offer, putting it out there for consideration and hoping you get lots of auditions.

Auditions & Messages

Audible will notify you by email when there is a new message or audition for your book.

Messages

Before posting an audition, sometimes a prospective producer will send you a message with a question. In this case, go to ACX.com, log in and click on New Messages. Read it, hit Reply, and type in your answer in the space provided for your answer above the message. Unlike other software, you will be able to hit "enter paragraph" without having the message delete or go out. When finished, hit Send Reply.

For now, you will correspond with producers in this fashion. Later you may exchange private email addresses, if you prefer. However, it is always a good idea to use the Audible messaging service for important agreements, details and/or changes made with your producer. In this way, Audible will have a record of it in case of any later problem or dispute.

Needless to say, you will write friendly messages with a certain amount of decorum.

Auditions

Here is where the fun work begins. Hopefully, one day you will receive an email from Audible notifying you that you have a ~~fish on the hook~~ ... er ... audition.

Remember how it felt the first time you held your new baby—your first published book? Hearing your words recorded is the same thrill.

Go to ACX.com and select New Auditions. Notice the choices: Title Not Posted, Open for Audition, Offers, In Production, Completed Projects and Programs. Select Open for Audition and scroll down.

Click on your title. A new page opens. If you have ever played a song or video on your computer, you will recognise a familiar looking time-bar with a tiny blue arrow, meaning play. Click the blue arrow repeatedly and you will see it toggle between the arrow and twin vertical lines, meaning play and pause. Make sure your speakers are on, and click the arrow once (or twice) to switch to the pause sign and make it play. You will hear the producer's voice reading your sample, as an orange/red bar progresses across the bar from left to right. On the far right of the bar you will see the number of seconds count up.

If it is not loud enough, look for a tiny orange/red speaker icon just to the right of those timing numbers. Click repeatedly just to the right of that speaker on some tiny little curved lines and you can raise or lower the volume to one of three different settings. Of course you can also adjust the volume on your computer in the normal fashion.

Anytime you want to repeat a particularly passage, simply click anywhere on the bar. The recording will jump to that spot and play forward. You may need to click Play again. You can return to the beginning by clicking at the far left spot in the bar. You may click Pause at any time, as well. Click Play and the recording will resume playing where it left off. No doubt you will listen to the recording many times, especially if you are lucky enough to receive multiple auditions from several different producers.

Note: If you run into any trouble repeating or moving through the recording, try closing out of the web site and entering again. In a worse-case scenario, simply reboot your computer.

You have the option to leave the audition as is, for now, in the Maybe section. But, eventually you will choose like or dislike. If you choose dislike, the producer will be notified that his audition was not the winner. As a courtesy, I like to write directly to the producer with an encouraging note. We authors know, only too well, how it feels to get those rejection letters. Even so, a kind rejection note is better than no reply at all.

There is a "Send Message to Producer" option next to the recording bar.

If you choose "Like" the audition will move from a "Maybe" into a new file with other "liked" auditions. Next time you open your ACX account, remember how you found it, under Projects.

Do not be alarmed if the audition you liked seems to have disappeared. Simply click on the cover icon. A new page opens. Look for the words Maybe, Like, and Dislike. You audition will be in the Like section. Click Like and it will open for you.

Choosing a Producer

Choosing your first producer is a crucial decision and sets the tone for all that is to come.

If you are looking for a split royalty, you may have none or just one audition. But, if you have indicated a cash offer of at least $50-$100 PFH—Per Finished Hour—hopefully, you will have accumulated several auditions in your 'Liked" file. Spend as much time as you need to listen and compare. After you narrow down your choices, you will want to investigate the semi-finalists on your liked producers' list. You can look at their Audible file where they will have posted a bio and a selection of samples from their work. (Find this by clicking on their name.) If this is an experienced producer, you can access their books on Amazon (Search Amazon by the producer's name) and listen to the retail samples of those books. Check out the sales ranking of the book. Enlist opinions from family members or friends. Sleep on it and listen again. Rank your favorites 1–2–3.

Most probably, the choice will come down to "good" vs. another "good." Each one is different, but wonderful. Other factors may come into play, such as price and experience. So, now you have done all you can. You must make a choice.

In case I must turn down a perfectly good producer, I feel I really owe that person a nice letter, giving some reasons, and positive suggestions. For instance, one woman had a young sounding voice and talked too fast for my "older" ears, like the younger generation is wont to do. I pointed out a few good things about her recording and suggested that she bid on some YA–Young Adult–novels.

In another case a man was good, but someone else appealed to me for that particular book. It was a subjective decision. I encouraged him to keep trying and to bid on another one of my books. He did and we settled a contract.

Make an Offer

It is possible to message back and forth with your favorite producer. Other conditions may be involved, which need to be discussed. In one case, my producer needed extra time. I revised my offer to allow a later final date.

In another case, we dickered over the price. I was thinking of $50 per finished hour and he couldn't work for less than $100. We finally settled on $75, but with the proviso that he would only work on the project between other jobs.

Eventually you must make a formal offer. Audible sets up a contract between the two of you. You can read the fine print, if you care to do so. Your offer details will include three items, 1.) The price per finished hour. 2.) The due date for the first 15 minutes. 3.) The due date for the finished product.

Price Per Finished Hour

The Audible program has already calculated the estimated number of hours in the finished recording based on the number of words in your book. (See note below.) The price you pay will be based on those figures. For instance, 5 hours and 15 minutes at $100 per finished hour will be $525. Consider this when you make your offer.

(Note: I assume you entered the number of words when you first entered details of your book. No doubt you know this, but, just in case, you can find the number of words at the bottom of your Word document. ACX makes an estimate based on that number. The final price is based on the actual end-product's length.)

Due Date for the First Fifteen Minutes

Once your producer accepts your offer you will post an upload, or email, the entire manuscript (depending on length). Here is where you really go to town with directions. The more you say, the better will be the outcome. One of my producers asked me to make a list of all the characters in the book, in order of appearance and importance, whether major, minor, supporting or inconsequential. He designed a different voice for each of the major characters. In some cases he consulted me for advice.

The producer will record the first fifteen minutes for your approval and post it on or before the date agreed upon in your contract. You will, then, listen to this recording. You may send the producer a message, making any comments, and/or asking for any changes. (More on that below.)

It is not unusual for circumstances to cause a delay. In this case you can agree to a new deadline by messaging back and forth.

At this point, you still have the option to back out of the contract. Once accepted, you click "Approved." This unlocks and allows the producer to go forward with the rest of the recording.

Locked/Unlocked

Once the producer posts his first fifteen minutes, the program becomes "locked" to him/her, meaning he cannot access it, even if you ask for changes. And so, in that unlikely event, you must "Approve" the first fifteen even if you do not approve. This will allow the producer to upload a new recording with the changes you requested.

There is a certain amount of flexibility between the two of you, to make side (gentlemen's) agreements. For example, my producer and I were debating the best type of "voice" for a certain character. He offered three different styles of voices. Did I want "smooth and sexy," "strong and determined," or a "Western drawl"? He was willing to record a sample in those three styles. I could choose one, or suggest something else.

And so by agreement, I "approved" the first fifteen-minute sample, even though we hadn't agreed on that particular vocal quality. My producer was then able to upload a recording of the three sample voices, reading the same paragraph. I chose number two, and he was able to delete and go on with recording Chapter One.

Final Due Date

A part of your offer to the producer is a final date for completion. Naturally we assume the producer will go forward with vigor, but just in case something happens, you can extend the final due date, as needed, by mutual agreement. Again, it is prudent to do this using the Audible messaging service, thus having a written record of the amended contract agreement.

In case you agree to an extension it is best to set a firm date. In a worst-case scenario, if the producer fails to finish the recording on time, even after repeated delays, you are released from the contract with no black mark on your record.

Creating a Cover

Meanwhile, the ACX.com website will request that you post a cover for your Audible book. It cannot be the same cover you used for your print book or eBook, but it should resemble that cover. In short, you need to create a new cover and upload it to the ACX site.

If you hired an artist to create your book cover, you may go back to that person and engage him/her to create an Audible cover. (Note: Next time you hire an artist to design your book cover, instruct him/her to create an Audible cover, too, at the same time.)

Otherwise, the only option remaining is to do-it-yourself. There are several kinds of software available for designing book-covers, and you may already have one on your computer. If you have Microsoft Office on your computer, it will have come bundled with Microsoft Publisher. If not, I recommend you search for book-cover software and see what you find.

The end result you will need is a square jpeg or jpg (picture) file. (Png or Tif is also acceptable.) Microsoft Publisher files end in the extension PUB. However, the software allows you to "Save As" a "JPEG File Interchange format (jpg)" which is exactly what you need. The final result should appear the same as a typical CD cover, but it must be larger.

When I set about to create my first Audible cover, I measured one of my CDs and decided to make the cover five inches square. After spending hours happily creating,

I tried to upload the finished file. Ha! It was rejected as being too small. (The minimum image size is 2400 X 2400 px 24 bit minimum. Make sense? ☺) In the end, I discovered that an eighteen-inch square picture file was acceptable. Of course, that was too big to fit on my computer display, but I worked around that problem by reducing the size in the "View" menu.

You can start by importing a picture of your eBook cover, which is, hopefully, on your computer. First, place your cursor in your document. Next, select "Import" or "Insert/Picture/from file. Move to the picture's file. Select the picture. Click Insert, or Save.

Otherwise, you can copy your cover off the Amazon page. Simply go to your book's Amazon sales page. Open up the largest size picture of your book cover. If you published it in eBook format, you can enlarge the cover by using the "Look inside" feature. Right-click on the picture, choose "Copy" from the menu. This will place the picture on your hidden clipboard. Now you can paste the picture into the Publisher document using your keyboard paste command. (Place your cursor in the document, then hold down the "Ctrl" key plus the "V" key.)

Next you can resize, crop, and move the cover picture to suit, allowing space to add the pertinent information, including the narrator and/or producer. For more details, see my booklet *How to Create a Picture Book.*

When satisfied with your creation, save it in your book's master file on your computer, and Save As on your backup thumb (flash) drive. Next, Save As again, this time select the jpg option. Now you are ready to upload the picture to your ACX.com file for this book.

Uploading Your Cover

Sign in to ACX.com and select "In Production." Select your book and select the blank, square space allowed for the cover. A command choice will open. It may say "Edit Cover Art" or "Upload Cover Art." Select this and a page will open with requirements and instructions. Read this and then click "Browse." A directory of your computer will open. Simply go to the place where you stored your cover picture. Click on it and click Save. Wait while it uploads and follow any additional instructions. Later, if you have changed the cover you may choose "Edit Cover Art" and repeat the uploading procedure.

Corrections and Changes

The contract with your producer calls for a date of final approval.

Once the entire recording is posted, the recording is "locked" again to the producer. The author may make two rounds of requests for changes. As the author, you will listen to the recording with as much care and close attention as you gave to proofreading your original book.

As you listen, make a list of the chapter, minute and second where you wish to make a change. Write out detailed and complete instructions and send them to your producer. (Audible has a downloadable form for this, if you care to use it.) This unlocks it, again, for the producer. He/she then records the requested changes and uploads the new recording.

You must listen a second time. By contract, you are allowed one more list of requested changes. In practice your producer may generously agree to more than two rounds of changes, but try not to abuse that offer.

After a third listen, you must either Approve or reject the recording. Bear in mind that any rejection should be carefully substantiated, lest you become labeled as "unreasonable," in which case, you would probably never get another decent offer.

After approving all the chapters, you may still decide to work on perfecting the Retail Sample. More on that later.

Downloading a Sample

Before you click on that final "Approve" you will want to download a recording of your book for your personal files. Why? It is the same reason that you should keep an original copy of your book and its cover–because you never know when you might need it. At this point, Amazon and Audible Inc. seem too big to fail, but there is no harm in saving your books and all of their versions.

External Storage

If this is too much data for your storage system, you will need an external storage device. I use a thumb drive (aka flash drive) which can be inserted into a USB port on my computer. (See *How to Move*, later.) Not all computers have a USB port. For those devices, there are other means of external storage. If you are using Microsoft Word, the software can easily access "One Drive." Since the topic of external drives is too big for this book, I found numerous articles on the subject by typing a question in an online search area. Wikipedia has an excellent article. Go to Wikipedia.org and search for External Storage.

Horror Stories

Why is it important to save our books, in their original versions, and their covers? Let me share a couple examples.

Firstly, on several occasions I have helped other authors restore and self-publish their books when the original publisher went out of business. It was not easy, because the authors had not saved the original file.

Secondly, my Audible producer called me one day with an urgent request, "Dorothy, by any chance did you save the recording of X novel? (One of my novels.) I lost the file to one of the chapters," he moaned. The poor chap had been looking everywhere. He makes audiobooks full-time. Imagine how many different recordings he had!

Was I able to save the day? You betcha'! In a few seconds I located the chapter in question, attached it to an email and sent it on its mission of mercy. I was a "heroine for a day."

How to Download

I try to wait until all the corrections have been made before I download the chapters to my computer. There is no need to keep downloading each revision.

After you have listened to a chapter, you will see a download button on the right side of each chapter listing. Click on it and watch for a small box to appear in the far bottom left corner of your screen. Inside the box, a counter will tick off the seconds as the chapter is downloading.

If you cannot see the box, try scrolling down and left, or reduce the size of your screen by using Ctrl plus -. (Hold down the Ctrl key while you hit the minus key. The screen will reduce once in size with each depression of the minus key.)

When finished you can return your screen to the right size by reversing the process, this time using Ctrl plus +. (Got it?)

Once you have located the box in question, it will show you when it is finished downloading. If you do nothing, the chapter will be in your Download file on your computer. But I like to go one step further and move the chapter onto a special external file which I have prepared.

Move your mouse over the box until you see the options: Save, Open, Show in file or Show in folder. Choose the Show option. Now your computer will show the file in the Download folder.

Now is a good time to change the name. Right clicking on the name will open an option list. Choose "Rename". Type in a new name. I use a short name of the novel followed by Ch __ (insert number). You can stop now, confident that the chapters will be grouped together in your Download file. However, I like to put the chapters on an external thumb drive.

In the meantime, I have selected a thumb drive that I use for all my Audible books and have inserted it into my computer's USB port. Probably when you first insert it a window will open showing the name of this drive. In my case it is "D" drive. But all your different drives have letter names.

How to Move

After you finish renaming the file, right-clicking on the name once more will reopen the menu. This time, you will select "Send to" with your left mouse. A new menu will open showing several places where you might choose to send this chapter. You will see that you could make a folder in your documents, for instance. However, in order to send it to your thumb drive you will see something toward the bottom of the list. It may say "Removable disk D", indicating a removable disk in the D Drive. Click on that option.

It may take a minute or so to move the chapter over to the D Drive. On my computer, a neat little window opens up with a little indicator showing how far it has progressed.

When finished, I move back to ACX.com and download the next chapter. I try to set aside an hour to do this job all at once, because each book recording takes a couple of tries before I remember how to do it. Also, I want to rename each chapter the exact same way so they line up in order in the same place. Once I get in the grove, it moves quickly.

There are other things you can do. You will see those options as you go along. For instance, instead of moving the chapters, you may want to cut and paste them. Or you may want to store them in more than one place. Or you may want to email a chapter to your mom.

When you are all finished, you can open your thumb drive and check out your work. All the chapters should be lined up neatly. However, if you made a typo or spelling error, you can rename them here. Sometimes something so small as an extra space or dot will cause a chapter to be out of order. Also, if you have more than one audible book on this thumb drive, you can create a folder for each book. It is an easy matter to drag and drop the chapters into the new folder.

Creating a New Folder

Open the thumb drive (or other external storage device) by clicking on it. You will find it listed under This PC/Devices and Drives. Mine is named "Removable Disk D." After you click on it you will find an icon along the top named "New Folder." Click "New Folder" to open a blank folder. Give the folder a new name by erasing the current name and typing in a new one.

(Note: If you are simply stymied and cannot locate the external drive, try right-clicking your window icon which will be located in the far corner of your display. A menu will open. Select "Device Manager" or something similar. A list will open showing every device on your computer.)

How to Drag and Drop

Now you should have your new folder plus a list showing every chapter. To drag a chapter into the correct folder, simply "grab" it by moving the curser over the title. While holding down the left mouse button, move the cursor over the correct folder. Release the left mouse button and the chapter will pop into the folder. Did you make a mistake? Try using the back "undo" arrow to reverse the command. Another option is to drag it back out of the folder. Or, finally, you can right click on it to open the "Send to" command again.

Relaxing the Rules, in Practice

As a practical matter, most of my producers upload a chapter at a time. As soon as it is ready they send me a quick message suggesting that I listen to the chapter and let them know if I find anything that needs changing. This is a useful thing to do when working with a long book. I was able to "proof" the recording as we went along, rather than having one huge job at the end. Also the text was still fresh in the producer's mind and easily fixed.

There was never an instance where I requested a big change in wording. But I often found vocal typos. Perhaps a word was mispronounced or recorded twice. Maybe I thought there needed to be a longer wait between scenes. Maybe the producer's voice slipped, somehow. Whatever.

Acting as an editor, after each chapter I sent a list of corrections to the producer. He fixed them, posted the changes and we were done with that chapter.

The recording systems allow the producers to change one word, and add or remove a space, for instance, without having to redo the entire recording.

Some Are Perfectionists

Some of my producers are perfectionists. These folks pronounce each word distinctly and then go over their recording with a fine-toothed comb before they upload it for me to hear. For instance, in one case I found only one vocal typo in the entire recorded book. All it amounted to was an incorrectly accented syllable in a long word. The producer was actually embarrassed that one had slipped through.

The other extreme was the producer who made a sensational and exciting recording, but it was full of vocal typos, repeated words and phrases, whole pages omitted, etc. In this case, I carefully listed each typo with the chapter, minute and second, the word or words and the corrections needed. The producer blissfully made the corrections as if it was a normal part of his routine. Usually the corrected copy was posted within a day or a few hours. We finished the book in record time. The final recording is great—one of the best—but was more work for me than some of the others.

You see, as the author, you are really a director working with the producer to make the finished product. You have a very important part to play, and the end work depends on your input.

The Retail Sample

The retail sample is the five minute excerpt that is made available to potential customers. You may wish to explore one of my Audible books on Amazon and listen to a retail sample It is similar to the "Look Inside" feature on your Amazon Kindle eBooks' sales pages. The customer can click on the words "Audible Sample" next to the tiny arrow underneath the image of the cover of your audible book. This is not easy to see for the inexperience shopper, and so you may need to help them find it.

One thing you can do is post an icon on your web page with a link to the retail sample. You will find several links on my web page, MercerPublications.com. Scroll down the Menu to "Talking Books." Open that page and click on any one of the covers you see. This will take you to the exact Amazon page where you can click on the words Audible Sample. Time permitting, go back to my web page and listen to several examples. You should notice an amazing variety in the voices, no two alike, but all are great.

Another thing I hope you will notice is the care with which we chose the excerpts to use for the retail sample. At first, the producer simply posted the first five minutes of Chapter One. He was more than willing to change that, according to my suggestions. In the non-fiction example, I opted to leave the sample as it was. In the fiction novels I spent hours listening to the recording and choosing excerpts that I thought would showcase the producer and make the book appealing to the prospective buyer. I did this with the same care that you use when choosing words to describe your eBook or to post on the back cover of your print version.

As I chose each selection I made a list of the chapter, the starting minute and second, and the ending minute and second. The total time allowance is five minutes. The list might look something like this:

Ch. 1, 12' 13" to 12' 45" =32 sec.

Ch. 7, 3' 14" to 4' 01" = 47 sec.   etc.

The list would continue until it totaled not quite 300 seconds, thus allowing time for a bit of space between segments.

Final Approval & Payment

When the producer uploads the last chapter and the retail sample, and after you are completely satisfied, you give your Final Approval. At this point the production is locked. It is up to you to make payment.

The amount will be posted in dollars and cents according to the exact hours and minutes in the finished product. You must pay the producer directly, and not through the Audible network. I write to the producer and inquire how he/she would like to be paid, either by Pay Pal, direct deposit, or by check.

After the producer receives payment, he/she notifies Audible that payment was received.

Now the audiobook goes to the Audible editing department. They will take two to three weeks (sometimes longer) to review the production to ascertain whether it meets their standards. They listen to the book and may request changes. Both the producer and the author are notified of any needed changes, but it is up to the producer to make those changes.

I have never had any requested changes, and so I can only assume that it can be handled smoothly. All the producers with whom I have dealt have wanted to establish a good reputation so that they could generate higher rates per hour. Thus, it behooves them to cooperate fully.

Joilè!

The happy day will arrive when you receive notice that Audible has approved of your creation and publishing will commence within a certain number of hours. Usually it shows up on Amazon soon. You may be surprised at the retail price. But you may also be surprised that the astute buyer can get your recording for free in a number of ways.

Marketing

Now that your Audible book is on Amazon.com, within a few days it will be connected with your book and eBook. If not, you can go to AuthorCentral.Amazon.com and claim your book, as follows:

Sign in with your Amazon ID and Password. Click Books. Scroll down to ascertain that all your book covers are listed. If you have more than one page of book covers, a control at the bottom of the page will allow you to go to the next page or show more pages. On each book the number of versions will show. Clicking the plus sign for each version will give you more details such as the publication date. Clicking on the cover will take you to the Amazon details for that title. Click on "View on Amazon" to go to the Amazon page for that title. Using the back arrow will navigate you back through the pages you have viewed.

If some titles or some versions are missing, click the button "Add more books" and follow the instructions. If you are still having trouble, click the Help button on the top right of the Books page. Sometimes the answer to your question is right there. Other times I use the "Contact Us" option to email the Service department. In a day or so I will receive an email in answer to my problem. I have always been helped courteously.

It is very exciting to see your Audible version advertised for sale. Click on the Audible Sample button to listen to a sample of your book. Notice the three ways a customer can buy it. 1.) Retail price 2.) Free with an Audible trial 3.) Free with an Audible membership. Sometimes there is a fourth offer–a bargain price if purchased with the eBook version.

Another part of Audible's promotion efforts is to give you, the author, a supply of Code Numbers. These Codes can be used for free or discounted downloads. You are encouraged to use them as prizes, or giveaways to promote sales.

A good way to promote your Audible book is to notify everyone of the free giveaway with a trial membership. Sometimes the trial period is for 30 days, during which time they may order one or two free Audible books. After that it is $14.65 a month. The exact details will be listed on your book's Amazon page. Sometimes the offer is a bit sweeter, up to 3 free months of membership and 3 free books. If you, as the author persuade anyone to enroll in the free membership at the same time as they order your Audible book, you will receive a $50 bonus from Audible.

What are some of the ways to notify everyone? Start with friends, relatives and people on your email list. Put notices on Twitter, Facebook and Linked In, your blog, your website, and any other groups you can join and not just once. Repeated notices will generate more sales.

ACX.com has marketing suggestions. Also, you may take advantage of their blog posts and ACX University which is a video service to sharpen your skills. Access to these helps is found on the ACX home page. Simply scroll down to view the curriculum.

Marketing is tedious work but keep at it. Soon you will receive the rewards.

Good luck!

Dear Reader.

Was this article helpful to you? Did it deliver as promised? If you liked this article, please do me favors:

- Please go to Amazon and leave a simple, but nice, five-star review. Go to any/all of these sites and search for Dorothy May Mercer
- Thanks a million.
-

  - US Amazon.com/ (Search for Dorothy May Mercer)
  - UK: Amazon.co.UK (Search for Dorothy May Mercer)
  - CA: Amazon.com.ca (Search for Dorothy May Mercer
  - AU: Amazon.com.au (Search for Dorothy May Mercer

  Not many folks will take the trouble to post a review, and even fewer will bother to copy and paste it in other marketplaces. You are truly one in a million! Three Cheers!
- If you purchased this book, I know you will not "return" it for a refund. Sometimes, customers do so, perhaps unaware that it puts a black mark on the author's record. Amazon keeps track of these things.
- If you used the Amazon library option, and borrowed this book, you may return it, now, and borrow it again, anytime. You may even buy it. Thank you!

While you are there, please consider buying/borrowing another book by Dorothy May Mercer. Or, you may consider the Want-to-Buy option and put several books on your "Add to Wish List." Amazon notices everything! Besides, this list makes a good suggestion list for your next birthday or anniversary wish list.

Another good option is the "Give as a Gift." Amazon sends a beautiful gift card to the recipient. You can add your own special message. Easy-Peezy.

Two easy ways to find all of the Dorothy May Mercer books:

1. Go to www.MercerPublications.com for links.

Tip: Look at the "How to For You" menu for 21 helpful books for authors and indie publishers.

2. Go to any Amazon site and search for Dorothy May Mercer.

Tip: There are seven Amazon pages for her books. The control at the bottom of the first page will navigate you to any page of her books.

Check out the latest at:

http://www.MercerPublications.com

Blog: http://mikemcbridenovels.blogspot.com/

Twitter: DorothyMMercer

Facebook: theSavageSurrogate

Email:info@MercerPublications.com

Thank You!

A bonus gift for you, just for reading this book"
Go to MercerPublications.com and scroll down to:

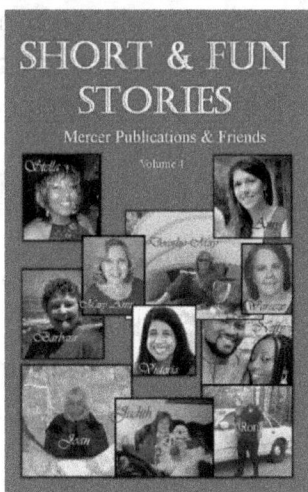

For a free E book, go to MercerPublications.com and click on the title, "Short & Fun Stories."

Thank you for purchasing this "How to For You" Series. We hope you enjoyed and found at least one helpful tip. Please encourage other writers by posting a short, positive review on the Amazon or other site where you purchased this book. Go to one or all of the following Amazon pages:

Amazon USA www.amazon.com
Amazon United Kingdom www.amazon.co.uk
Amazon Canada www.amazon.ca
Amazon Brazil www.amazon.br
Amazon Mexico www.amazon.com.mx
Amazon France www.amazon.fr
Amazon Italy www.amazon.com.it
Amazon Denmark www.amazon.de
Amazon India www.amazon.in
Amazon Australia www.amazon.com.au

And while you are there please consider another book or booklet by this author. Links to all of these books can be found at www.mercerpublications.com

The complete "How to For You" series of booklets for improving writers.

1. "How to Write Sentences and Paragraphs" *in Your Novel,* eBook
2. "How to Install a Link in Your Document" eBook
3. "How to Sell Your eBook Using Amazon Free Days," eBook
4. "How to Prepare Your Book for Kindle" eBook
5. "How to Fix Errors in Your Document," *Find and Replace Globally,* eBook
6. "How to Use Your Book for Free Ads" eBook
7. "How to Design and Format Your Paragraphs" –Two Editions, –Two Editions, eBook and Print
8. "How to Design a Kindle eBook Cover" –Two Editions, eBook and Print
9. "How to Add an Interactive Table of Contents" eBook

10. "How to Format Your Book, for Publishing"– Two Editions, eBook and Print
11. "How to Edit a Book," With a Friend–Two Editions, eBook and Print
12. "How to Write Great Dialog"–Two Editions, eBook and Print
13. "How to Market Your Book," Marketing 101– Two Editions, eBook and Print
14. "Book Marketing Bargain Bundle," Three For One, Includes #13, #6 & #3-Print Edition Only
15. "Book Covers Bargain Bundle: Do Your Own and Save," –Two Editions, eBook and Print
16. "Formatting Bargain Bundle," Two for One, (Includes #10 and #7) Print Edition Only
17. "How to Register ISBNs & Copyrights" –Two Editions, eBook and Print
18. "How to Self-Publish" *Your Book* . –Two Editions, eBook and Print
19. "How to Write Fiction: The Basics," –Two Editions, eBook and Print
20. "How to Create a Picture Book" –Two Editions, eBook and Print
21. "How to Get an Audible Version "*of Your Book*– Second Edition, eBook and Print

Now in Audible Book (Talking Books) Version:
"Leon and Esther"
"Let's Talk" a Black/White Dialog in the US & the UK
"Cynthia & Dan, Cyber War"
"Car oo6 Responding" English and Spanish
"The Cocaine Chase" English and Spanish

"The Golden Coin" English and Spanish
"The Cartel Wars" English and Spanish
"The Gang Bust"
"The Fairfax Fix"
 "The Arlington Alias"
"The Savage Surrogate"
"Fran and Max, The Bungalow"
"Mary Beth and Sammy, Rolling Thunder"
"Nate, the Search"
"EMP Honeymoon"
"Civil War Experiences of a German Emigrant"
"The Joys and Sorrows of an Emigrant Family"

The McBride Series of Action Novels, Starring Det. Lt. Michael J. McBride Jr.
A Series for Those Looking for Good Clean Cop Stories. Now in English and Spanish.

"Car oo6 Responding" (Proceeds to Police Charities.
"The Cocaine Chase"
"The Immigrant and the Golden Coin"
"The Cartel Wars"
"The Gang Bust"

The Washington McBride Novels, Starring Senator Mike McBride, his wife Juliette, featuring his bodyguard, Cynthia Patterson: in Print, eBook & Audible versions:

"The Fairfax Fix".
"The Arlington Alias"
"The Savage Surrogate"

The McBride Suspense/Romances: Print, eBook & Audible
"Fran and Max" *The Bungalow.*
"Cynthia and Dan" *Cyber War*
"Mary Beth and Sammy," *Rolling Thunder* (YA)
"Nate" *the Search*
"EMP Honeymoon" *Kelly and Tom*

Photo-Travel books by Dorothy May Mercer, author, and Dave Mercer, photographer:

- "Alaska and Back" With Dave and Dorothy.
- "Africa and Back" With Dave and Dorothy
- "Hawaii and Back," Vol. 1 Kauai" With Dave and Dorothy
- "Hawaii and Back," Vol 2, Maui, With Dave and Dorothy
- "Hawaii and Back," Vol 3, Oahu, With Dave and Dorothy
- "Hawaii and Back," Vol 4, Kauai Via SFO, With Dave and Dorothy
- "Niagara and Back," With Dave and Dorothy

More books by Dorothy May Mercer:

"Leon and Esther," an historical Christian love story.
"Stories I Haven't Told," an auto biography

Other Author's Books published by Mercer Publications & Ministries, Inc.:

- "Let's Talk" a Black/White Dialog in the US & the UK
- "Short & Fun Stories" Vols 1 & 2 by fourteen authors.
- "Stormy Affair," a Romance, by Netty Ejike
- "Sensual Bond," 5 Part Saga Series, by Netty Ejike
- "He Called Her Hat," That Tough Little Lady, Amusing Historical Biography, by Myron C. McDonald
- "Notes From John," Messages from Beyond, by Marcia McMahon
- "Remember How Much I Love You," Romantic Suspense, by Dale L. Williams, M.D.
- "The Inheritance From Hell," True Drama, by R.D. Margot
- "Ascension Teachings," With Archangel Michael, by Marcia McMahon
- "Mary Magdalene Speaks," the Holy Grail, the Bloodline, and Secrets of the Divine Feminine, by Marcia McMahon
- "Gems", by Nancy S. Calumet
- "Heaven-Sent Love Letters," Between tom in Heaven and Nancy on Earth, by Nancy S. Calumet
- "Him and Her," A Story About survival in the Arctic, by Gerald Kinsey
- "Civil War Experiences of a German Emigrant," by 1st Lt. Joseph Ruff
- "The Joys and Sorrows of an Emigrant Family," by 1st Lt. Joseph Ruff

Thanks, Again.
See you soon, in another book.

Dorothy May Mercer, Author Extraordinaire

Have a wonderful day!